DAVID T. LITTLE

AND THE SKY WAS STILL THERE

for violin with effects and backing track

HENDON MUSIC

BOOSEY & HAWKES

DISTRIBUTED BY

HAL•LEONARD®
7777 W. BLUEMOUND RD. P.O. BOX 13819 MILWAUKEE, WI 53213

www.boosey.com
www.halleonard.com

Commissioned by Todd Reynolds

Developed in collaboration with Todd Reynolds
Ableton Live programming by David T. Little
Mixed by David T. Little and Todd Reynolds
Video by R. Luke Dubois (2011)
Story by Amber Ferenz from a conversation with the composer.
Additional text by Utah Phillips, courtesy of Democracy NOW

The world premiere recording of *and the sky was still there* is available
on Todd Reynolds' *Outerborough* (Innova Recordings #741)

PROGRAM NOTE

Written in 2010 for violinist Todd Reynolds, *and the sky was still there* tells the story of an old friend, Amber Ferenz, and the epiphany that led her to embrace her true self, confront the US Army, and accept a dishonorable discharge under the Army's Don't Ask Don't Tell policy. Amber tells her own story in this work, while the violin plays along, providing a sometimes-somber, sometimes-whimsical sub-text. Amber's story, though unique, represents a struggle we all face on some level, whether to conform to cultural expectations, or defy them in pursuit of greater truths.

– David T. Little

TEXT

text by Amber Ferenz

The first thing I remember, after getting through all the military initial processing, at the, what's called the MEPS center—um, that's the initial entry point, mine was in Charlotte, North Carolina—was a lot of standing around and a lot of yelling. We stood and stood and stood. We stood in lines because. We stood in lines for no reason. We stood in line to eat. We stood in line to go places. We stood in line to give blood, to get shots, to get our clothes. We stood in line just for the sheer joy of standing in line. And in those lines there was no talking. There was very little movement. We, we hadn't started basic training yet, we were still doing what is called "reception," uh, before the actual training takes place. And, I think that whole point of reception, besides all those initial processing things, like getting all those appointments taken care of, was to learn how to stand in line.

—

People were kicking me in the face. People were standing on my hands. People were, crawling practically right over the top of me, because we were all trying to get across this field, as you would if you were actually in combat and crawling you would want to get across that wide open space as fast as you…could. So, that's what we were doing.
I felt then the absolute impersonality of the military. I was only there as a weapon-toter. I was not there for my mind, for my skills, for any of the fabulous things that are me. I was there only as a body with a gun.

—

Living closeted in the military is unbelievably difficult. (She was in the Navy, I was in the Army). You have to ask as if nothing is wrong when people bash on gays all around you. You have to sort of "go with it" or it will come down upon you, too. (We were in Arabic class together. Um, we fell for each other really, really hard.)
If you tell, you get an honorable discharge. If they ask, and you tell, you get a dishonorable discharge.

—

Yes, I joined the Army.
Some people learn things the hard way,
But at least then you never forget it. *

—

But all of a sudden, I was too tired to get out of my car. And I was sitting there, looking across the flight-line—there was a chain-link fence in front of my car that I had parked up against—and the sun was coming in through the front window, and I felt very warm and very cozy, and I could see the dust motes in my car in the sunlight, and it was beautiful. And I'm looking at the fence, and the sky, and the flight-line, and being exhausted, and it was like everything stopped. Time just stopped. The dust motes hung suspended.
And I heard a voice that said to me: If you care about the state of your soul, if you care about anything at all, if you want to continue to b e a good person: Get out. You don't have much time. Get out. Get out, now!
And then the dust motes started up again. And the sky was still there, and the chain-link fence…but I had changed. I was done. I had quit. In that moment I understood that I needed to get out of the Army.

—

They sent me off to Sergeant school just after the New Year. And, I went. I told my Platoon Sergeant that I didn't want to go, but they said, you have to. (…) And we're all told, if you have any reason why you want to go home, speak up now or hold on to it. …and I told him.

—

To transition back to civilian life I decided to go hiking. My lover and I hit the Appalachian trail. I spent about three months out in the woods, and watched spring happen all around me, and I tried to figure out what I was gonna do next.

* *additional text by Utah Phillips, courtesy of Democracy NOW*

TECH REQUIREMENTS

Ableton Live 9 (or later) is required to run the electronic component of this work. This electronic component will be provided by the publisher in the form of an Ableton project file, which contains prerecorded audio, automated effects processing, and an optional click track.

Though the performer may choose to use an electric violin, an acoustic violin with transducer setup (or instrument mic) is preferred. In either case, the instrument must run through an audio interface, into a computer running Ableton Live, then out to the sound system. Please see the tech rider included with the files for complete instructions on set-up and execution. A sound engineer is highly recommended for performance.

Duration: ca. 8 minutes

Performance materials are available from the Boosey & Hawkes Rental Library

Contact usrental@boosey.com for more information

Playing Score

for Todd Reynolds

and the sky was still there

DAVID T. LITTLE
(2010)

story by
AMBER FERENZ

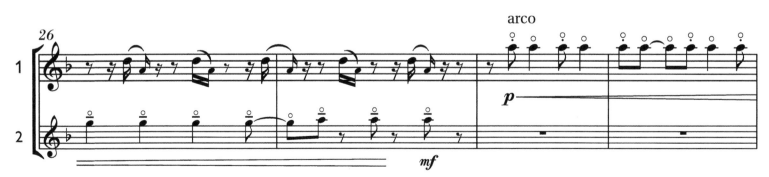

979-0-051-80215-9

Printed 2018

"People were kicking
me in the face"

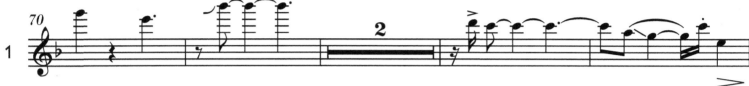

81 "Living closeted"

96 "Yes, I joined the army"

V.S.

BLANK FOR PAGE TURN

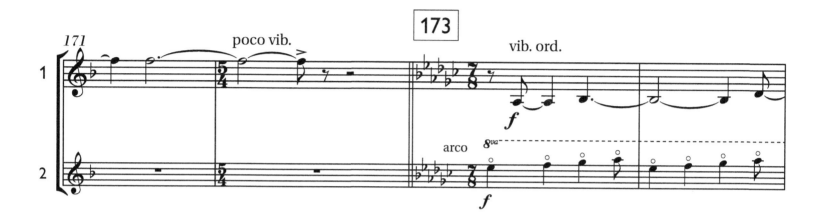

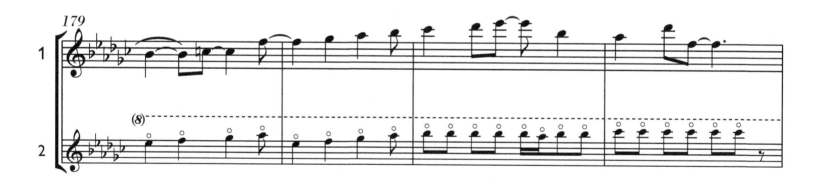

199

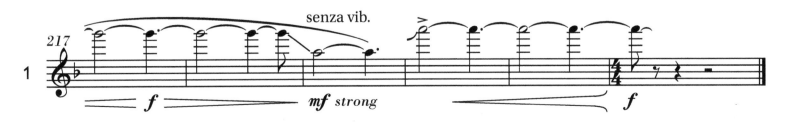